My Big Book of
ANIMALS

This edition published by Lorenz Books

Lorenz Books is an imprint of Anness Publishing Limited
Hermes House
88-89 Blackfriars Road
London SE1 8HA

ISBN 0 7548 0227 2

A CIP catalogue record for this book is available from the British Library.

Publisher: Joanna Lorenz
Editorial Consultant: Jackie Fortey
Natural History Consultant: Michael Chinery
Designer: Joy Fitzsimmons

Printed in Hong Kong/China

© Anness Publishing Limited 1994, 1999
1 3 5 7 9 10 8 6 4 2

My Big Book of
ANIMALS

Written by Jenny Vaughan
Illustrated by Ann Savage

LORENZ BOOKS

CONTENTS

CONTENTS

ALL ABOUT ANIMALS

There are millions of different kinds of animals in the world. They live in all sorts of different places and they all do different things. Some are hunters, some eat plants, some can swim, and some can fly, and some can run very fast.

All the different kinds of animals belong to two main groups. One is the group of animals with backbones. The other is the group without backbones.

The animals with backbones are fish, birds, reptiles, mammals, and amphibians.

Mammals usually have fur and warm bodies and their young drink milk. You are a mammal. So is this bear.

Birds have warm bodies, feathers and wings, but some birds cannot fly. They lay eggs.

Reptiles have dry scaly skins. Most reptiles lay eggs. Their bodies are only warm when they have been in a warm place.

WHERE DO all these different animals live?

Some live in our fields and farms,

some live in woods and forests,

others live in oceans, lakes and rivers.

8

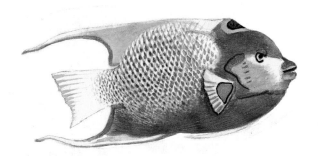

Fish live in water and breathe through gills. They usually have scaly skins. Most fish lay eggs.

Amphibians, like this frog, lay their eggs in water. The young live in water. Adults live in water and on land.

Many of the animals without backbones are very small. People sometimes call them 'minibeasts'. But some, such as octopuses and squid, can be large.

Insects always have six legs. Butterflies, beetles and flies are all insects.

Molluscs are a group of animals which usually have shells and no legs. Snails are molluscs. So are mussels and oysters.

Spiders have eight legs. There are many kinds of spiders. They are related to scorpions.

Lobsters and crabs are called **crustaceans.** They have lots of legs and hard, crusty shells.

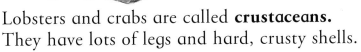

This book will show you many different kinds of animals and how they suit the places they live in.

Some live in hot, dry places,

some like hot, wet places,

and others are found in very cold places.

ANIMALS IN OUR HOME

People all over the world keep pets. We feed our pets and care for them. Some pets do useful jobs for us. Cats catch mice, and dogs can scare away burglars. But mostly, we keep pets just because we like them.

Rabbits usually live in a hutch. They eat grass and other plants.

Cats are meat-eaters, and people usually buy them food in tins.

Guinea pigs need a place to play, and somewhere cosy to sleep.

HOW DO we look after pets? Cats may need grooming, especially if they have long hair. They need food, and somewhere to sleep.

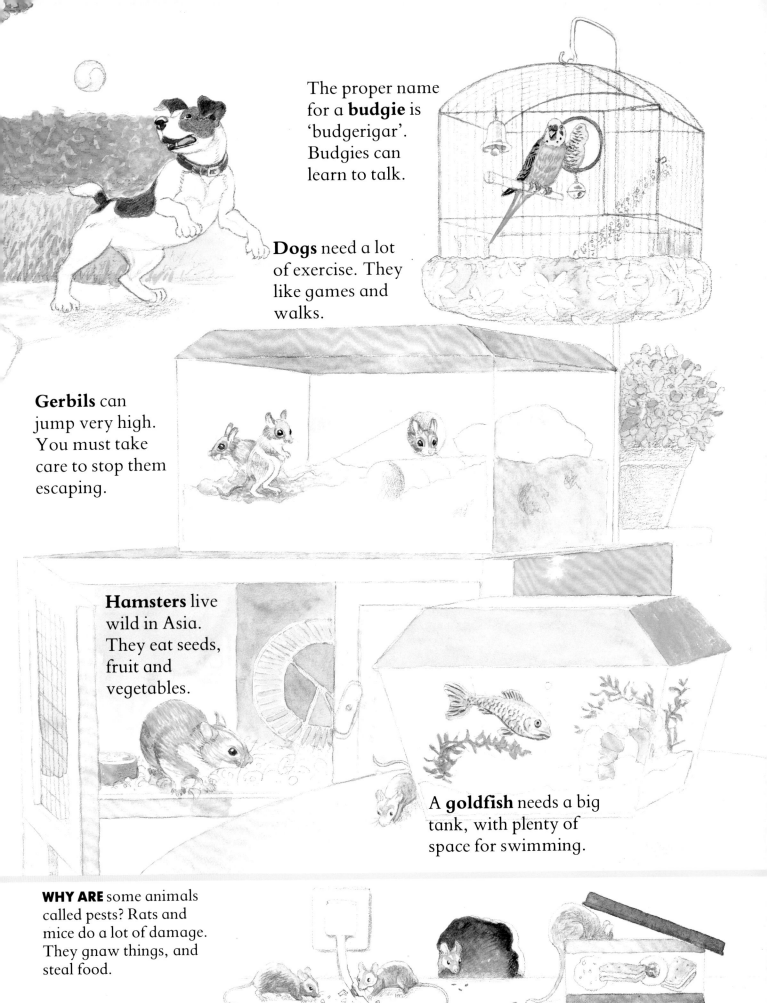

The proper name for a **budgie** is 'budgerigar'. Budgies can learn to talk.

Dogs need a lot of exercise. They like games and walks.

Gerbils can jump very high. You must take care to stop them escaping.

Hamsters live wild in Asia. They eat seeds, fruit and vegetables.

A **goldfish** needs a big tank, with plenty of space for swimming.

WHY ARE some animals called pests? Rats and mice do a lot of damage. They gnaw things, and steal food.

11

WORKING ANIMALS

Some kinds of animals work for people. Long ago, before there were cars, animals were used to carry heavy loads and to pull carts. Some animals still work in this way. Farmers keep animals because they give us meat, or other food such as eggs and milk.

In Asia, people milk **yaks** and use them to carry loads.

Farmers keep **sheep** for their wool. We use this to make cloth and sweaters.

Cows give us milk. A young cow is called a calf.

Donkeys are strong. They can pull carts and carry loads.

Chickens give us eggs to eat.

Ducks like to live near water. Young ducks are called ducklings.

HOW DO dogs help us? These sheep dogs are rounding up sheep. They can drive them to another field. The farmer shouts, or whistles, to tell the dogs what to do.

Camels are desert animals. They can go many days without food or water.

People from the mountains of South America use **llamas** to carry heavy loads.

Turkeys are big birds. They make a noise that sounds like "Gobble-gobble-gobble!"

Goats can eat very tough leaves and grass. Farmers keep goats for their milk.

Pigs like to dig in the soil with their snouts. Young pigs are called piglets.

People ride **horses**. Some large horses pull carts or ploughs. Young horses are called foals.

In snowy countries, people sometimes use teams of dogs called huskies to pull sledges. The dogs are strong and quick. The people shout to the dogs to tell them which way to go.

13

WOODLAND ANIMALS

Woods and forests are home to many
kinds of animals. Some like woodlands,
others live in the dark pine forests,
and some can live in both. The animals
in this picture live in the woods, forests
and countryside of northern Europe.

The **pine
marten** hunts
birds, steals eggs
and eats berries.

Red squirrels
live in pine forests
and woodlands.
They eat seeds
and nuts.

The **tawny
owl** hunts at
night, for mice
and other
small animals.

Wild cats are
bigger than pet
cats and have
thicker coats.

HOW DO toads breed? They
lay eggs, called toadspawn,
in water. Little black
tadpoles hatch from the
eggs. They look like fish,
but they slowly turn into
little toads.

spawn

tadpoles

young toads

14

Woodpeckers make holes in tree bark, and eat the insects they find there.

Wild boar search around beneath the trees, looking for roots, fallen fruit and fungi.

Fallow deer live in woodlands. The male has big bony antlers on his head.

A **fox** can live almost anywhere - in woods, the countryside and even in towns.

Badgers live underground. They come out at night to find food.

Toads hide all day and hunt at night, for slugs and snails.

Hedgehogs live in woods, fields and gardens. They eat insects.

HOW DO the hedgehog's prickles help keep it safe? When the hedgehog is afraid, it curls into a ball. Other animals leave it alone, because they do not want a mouthful of prickles.

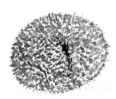

MORE WOODLAND ANIMALS

All these animals live in the woods and forests of North America. Some live in the northern pine forests. Others prefer the woodlands, further south. Some are hunters and some are plant-eaters. Some, such as bears, will eat almost anything.

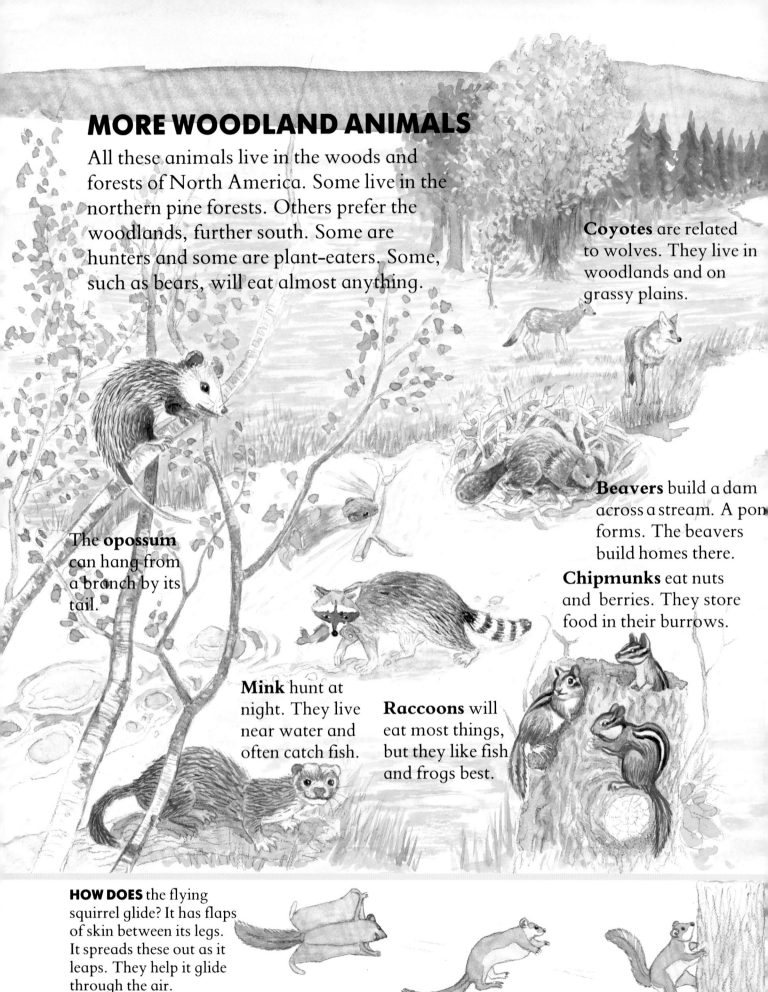

Coyotes are related to wolves. They live in woodlands and on grassy plains.

Beavers build a dam across a stream. A pon forms. The beavers build homes there.

Chipmunks eat nuts and berries. They store food in their burrows.

The **opossum** can hang from a branch by its tail.

Mink hunt at night. They live near water and often catch fish.

Raccoons will eat most things, but they like fish and frogs best.

HOW DOES the flying squirrel glide? It has flaps of skin between its legs. It spreads these out as it leaps. They help it glide through the air.

16

Wolverines live in northern forests. They hunt other animals, such as deer.

This squirrel can glide so well that it is called a **flying squirrel**.

Black bears hunt deer sometimes. They also eat eggs, fruit and berries.

The **bobcat's** spotted coat makes it hard to see among the trees.

Porcupines have spines called quills. These protect them from other animals.

Blue jays live in northern forests, but fly south in winter.

Wild turkeys are related to the tame ones that live on farms.

HOW DO blue jays help plant new trees? They bury acorns, so they can eat them later. But they do not find them all and some start to grow.

GRASSLAND ANIMALS

These animals live on the savanna, the grassy plains of Africa. Some eat grass or leaves from trees. Others are hunters. Many grassland animals can run fast, to catch food or escape from danger. They often have coats the colour of dry grass, to make them hard to see.

Giraffes are so tall they can nibble leaves at the tops of trees.

Lions live in groups called prides. They are fierce hunters.

Ostriches cannot fly, but they can run at 70 kilometres an hour.

Hippopotamuses spend all day in water. At night, they come out and eat grass.

Puff adders are poisonous snakes. They swell up when they are angry.

HOW DO lions hunt? The lionesses surround a herd of zebra and pounce on one of them. Then the lions, cubs and lionesses can all eat.

Vultures eat the remains of creatures killed by lions and other hunters.

When a **springbok** sees danger it jumps, to warn the rest of the herd.

African elephants eat bushes and grass. They live in groups called herds.

Jackals are a kind of wild dog. They live and hunt in family groups.

Oxpeckers eat the biting insects that live on the skin of buffalos.

Buffaloes are big and keep cool by lying in the mud.

Vervet monkeys leap through the trees, making a lot of noise.

HOW DO animals feed in the same part of the savanna? The giraffe eats from the tree-top. The gerenuk nibbles leaves lower down. The gazelle eats the grass beneath the trees.

19

MOUNTAIN ANIMALS

Many different kinds of animals live in the mountains. Some live among the trees on the lower slopes. Others live higher up, on grassy and rocky slopes. The animals in this picture live in the mountains of Asia.

Snow leopards hunt goats and other animals. They are found on high, rocky slopes.

Markhors are a kind of wild goat. They are good climbers.

Takins are like oxen. They live among the bushes growing high up in the mountains.

Himalayan black bears are hunters, but they also eat roots and berries.

HOW DO mountain animals climb on rocks and snow? They have special kinds of feet. Snow leopards and red pandas have wide, hairy feet to help them walk on snow and ice.

20

Griffon vultures soar above the mountains, looking for dead animals to eat.

Argalis live in the high plateaus of Tibet. They are a kind of wild sheep.

Most **yaks** are kept by people, but there are a few wild ones left.

Langur monkeys live in mountain forests and leap from tree to tree.

Red pandas eat berries and small animals.

The **Bhutan glory** butterfly only shows its bright colours when an enemy gets close.

HOW DO the animals keep warm in winter? Marmots spend winter hibernating (sleeping deeply) in their burrows. Takins, and other animals, move to warmer, lower slopes. Yaks' coats are so thick that they do not mind cold weather.

21

DESERT ANIMALS

Deserts are difficult places for animals to live. There is not much water and few plants grow. The animals in this picture live in the Sahara desert, in Africa. Here, the days are burning hot but the nights are very cold.

These **wild asses** (or donkeys) are related to tame donkeys.

The **addax** has specially wide hooves, to help it walk on sand.

The **sand cat** hunts small desert animals, such as the jerboa.

The **desert hedgehog** eats small animals like insects and scorpions.

Jerboas eat grass and seeds. They can jump high in the air to escape enemies.

WHY DOES this camel look so thin? It has not had anything to eat or drink for days. But as soon as it drinks, it looks fat and well again.

22

Camels' thick coats help keep them warm at night and cool by day.

Sandgrouse fly across the desert every day, looking for water to drink.

Parts of the Sahara have steep mountains, where **Barbary sheep** live.

Fennec foxes have huge ears. These help them hear the faintest sounds.

Monitor lizards steal eggs and hunt birds, other lizards and snakes.

Scorpions have poison stings in their tails. These can kill other animals.

HOW DO young sandgrouse drink? Their parents soak their own feathers with water and fly back to the nest. The young can drink water drops from the feathers.

ANIMALS IN COLD PLACES

In the far north, it is so cold that no trees will grow. This area is called the tundra. Further south, there are forests, but even here, winters are cold and very long. Only a few kinds of animals can live in these cold places.

Polar bears good swimm... They hunt ot... animals, espe...

Walruses live in the icy seas. They eat shellfish from the sea bed.

Arctic hares must watch out for hunters such as foxes and wolves.

Snowy owls hunt by day and night. They catch lemmings and other animals.

Lemmings eat plants. In winter, they make tunnels under the snow.

In summer, **Arctic ground squirrels** store food. They eat it in winter.

WHY DO animals in cold places grow white coats in winter? The hare changes colour to help it hide from enemies. The stoat changes colour to help it hide while it is hunting.

Arctic hare

winter

summer

Stoat

summer

winter

Reindeer eat moss and other tundra plants. They move south for the winter.

seals.

Wolves live and hunt in the tundra and northern forests.

Musk oxen have very long hair, to keep them warm in winter.

Arctic foxes have thick coats so they can live in very cold places.

The **lynx** is a big cat that lives in the northern forests.

The **sable** lives in the forests. It has a beautiful coat.

HOW DOES the Arctic fox find food in winter? In summer, when there are more animals to hunt, it hides some of the prey it has killed. It returns to eat it later in the year.

25

RAINFOREST ANIMALS

Rainforests are amazing places. There are tall trees, thick creepers and hundreds of different kinds of plants and animals. Some of the animals live up in the trees, and others stay in the shadows on the forest floor.

Jaguars are hunters. Their spots make them hard to see in the forest.

Macaws make holes in trees. They build their nests there.

Sloths spend almost all their lives hanging upside down in trees.

The **anaconda** is a huge snake. It lives near water.

WHY DO sloths often look quite green? This is not because they have green coats, but because tiny green plants called algae grow on their fur.

algae on fur

Howler monkeys live high in tree-tops. They make very loud noises.

The **emerald tree boa's** green colour helps it hide among the leaves.

Marmosets are the world's smallest monkeys.

Young **hoatzin** birds have claws on their wings. They use these for climbing.

Armadillos have hard backs, and huge claws, which they use for digging.

Tapirs live beneath the trees and eat plants that grow near rivers.

Capybaras are like giant guinea pigs. They live in water and on land.

The **toucan's** beak is enormous. It is very light and strong.

WHERE DO the animals live? Some birds and bats live in the tree-tops. Monkeys, sloths and tree frogs live among the branches. Fewer animals live on the forest floor.

Tree-tops

Branches

Forest floor

27

ANIMALS OF THE OCEAN

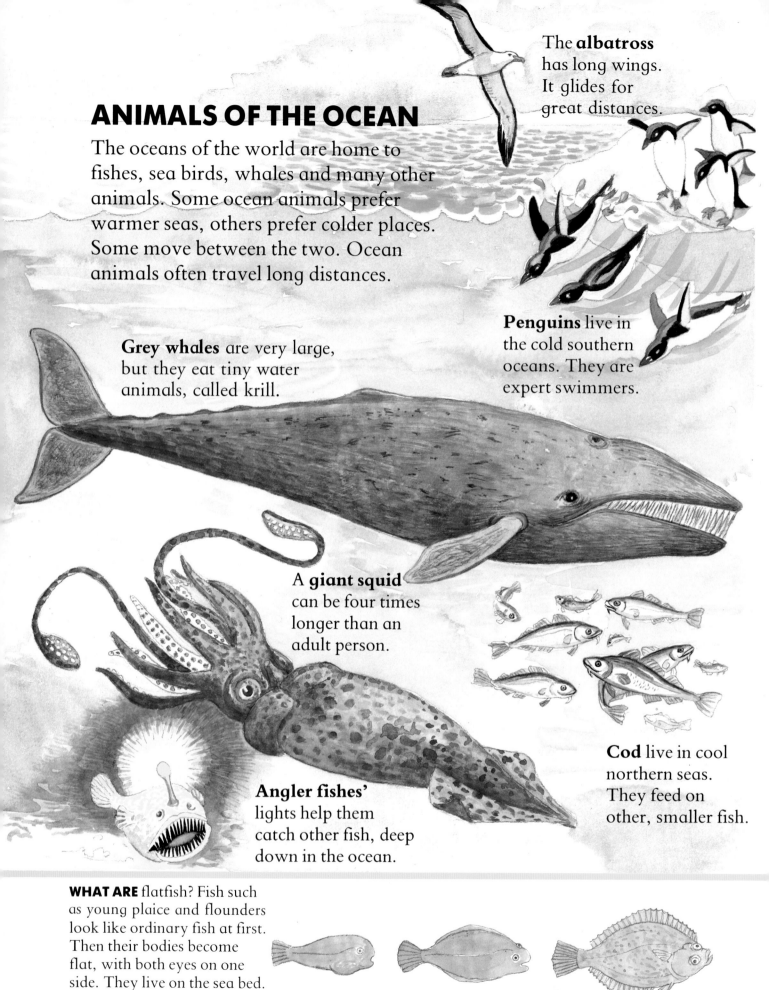

The oceans of the world are home to fishes, sea birds, whales and many other animals. Some ocean animals prefer warmer seas, others prefer colder places. Some move between the two. Ocean animals often travel long distances.

The **albatross** has long wings. It glides for great distances.

Penguins live in the cold southern oceans. They are expert swimmers.

Grey whales are very large, but they eat tiny water animals, called krill.

A **giant squid** can be four times longer than an adult person.

Cod live in cool northern seas. They feed on other, smaller fish.

Angler fishes' lights help them catch other fish, deep down in the ocean.

WHAT ARE flatfish? Fish such as young plaice and flounders look like ordinary fish at first. Then their bodies become flat, with both eyes on one side. They live on the sea bed.

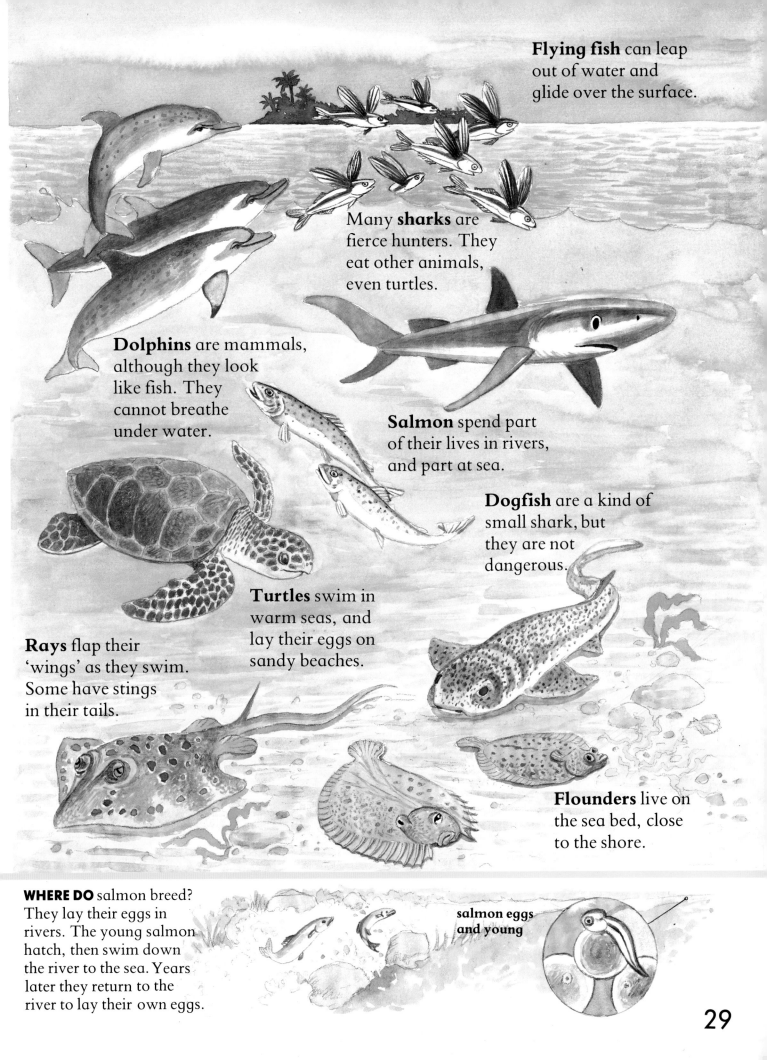

Flying fish can leap out of water and glide over the surface.

Many **sharks** are fierce hunters. They eat other animals, even turtles.

Dolphins are mammals, although they look like fish. They cannot breathe under water.

Salmon spend part of their lives in rivers, and part at sea.

Dogfish are a kind of small shark, but they are not dangerous.

Rays flap their 'wings' as they swim. Some have stings in their tails.

Turtles swim in warm seas, and lay their eggs on sandy beaches.

Flounders live on the sea bed, close to the shore.

WHERE DO salmon breed? They lay their eggs in rivers. The young salmon hatch, then swim down the river to the sea. Years later they return to the river to lay their own eggs.

salmon eggs and young

LIFE ON A CORAL REEF

Coral reefs are found in the warm seas of the world. Coral reefs are made up of the skeletons of millions of tiny coral animals. There are many different colours and shapes of coral. Brightly coloured fish swim among the corals.

The **lionfish** is beautiful, but it has poison spines on its back.

Giant clams are huge shellfish. They can be one metre across.

The **crown of thorns starfish** eats corals and destroys coral reefs.

The **mandarin fish** hides among the corals and eats smaller fish.

HOW DOES a coral reef grow? Each tiny coral animal grows layers of hard coral underneath itself. Gradually a mound of coral builds up.

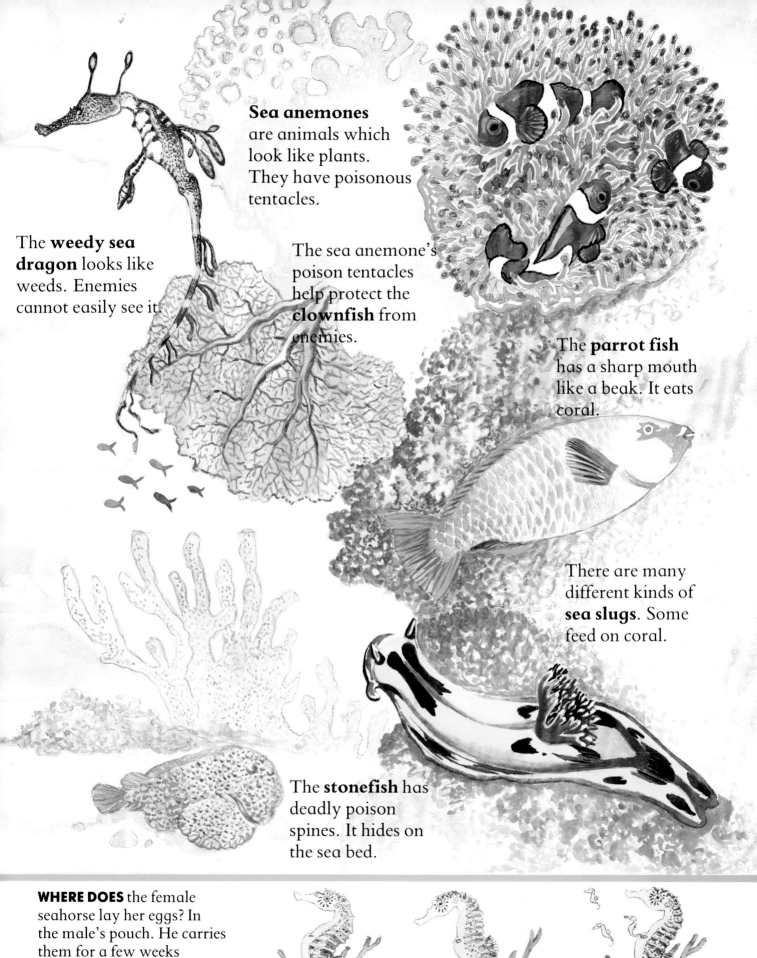

Sea anemones are animals which look like plants. They have poisonous tentacles.

The **weedy sea dragon** looks like weeds. Enemies cannot easily see it.

The sea anemone's poison tentacles help protect the **clownfish** from enemies.

The **parrot fish** has a sharp mouth like a beak. It eats coral.

There are many different kinds of **sea slugs**. Some feed on coral.

The **stonefish** has deadly poison spines. It hides on the sea bed.

WHERE DOES the female seahorse lay her eggs? In the male's pouch. He carries them for a few weeks with the pouch shut. When the eggs hatch, the pouch opens and the young are born.

LIFE ON THE SEASHORE

Most seashore animals are small. Some live on rocks. Others bury themselves in sand. Many seashore animals have shells, so they are called shellfish. The birds you see on the seashore are often looking for shellfish and other animals to eat.

Seals catch fish, out at sea. They come ashore to have their pups.

Limpets stick to the rocks. They eat seaweed that grows there.

Starfish eat shellfish. They use their arms to pull the shellfish open.

Shrimps are tiny, but they catch and eat even tinier animals.

Mussels live together in large groups. They cling on to rocks.

CAN A starfish grow a new arm? Most starfish have five arms. If a starfish loses an arm, it can grow a new one to take its place.

Oystercatchers do not catch oysters. But they eat other kinds of shellfish.

After a **cormorant** has been fishing, it stretches out its wings to dry.

Jellyfish float in the sea. Sometimes they are washed on to the beach.

As it grows, a **crab** sheds its shell and grows a new one.

Hermit crabs live in shells that used to belong to whelks and other shellfish.

A **sea urchin** has a hard shell, covered in spines.

Lugworms burrow into the sand and swallow it to eat tiny creatures and plants that live there.

HOW DO seabirds keep their eggs on rocky cliffs? The eggs are more pointed at one end than ordinary eggs. This shape helps stop the eggs from rolling into the sea.

33

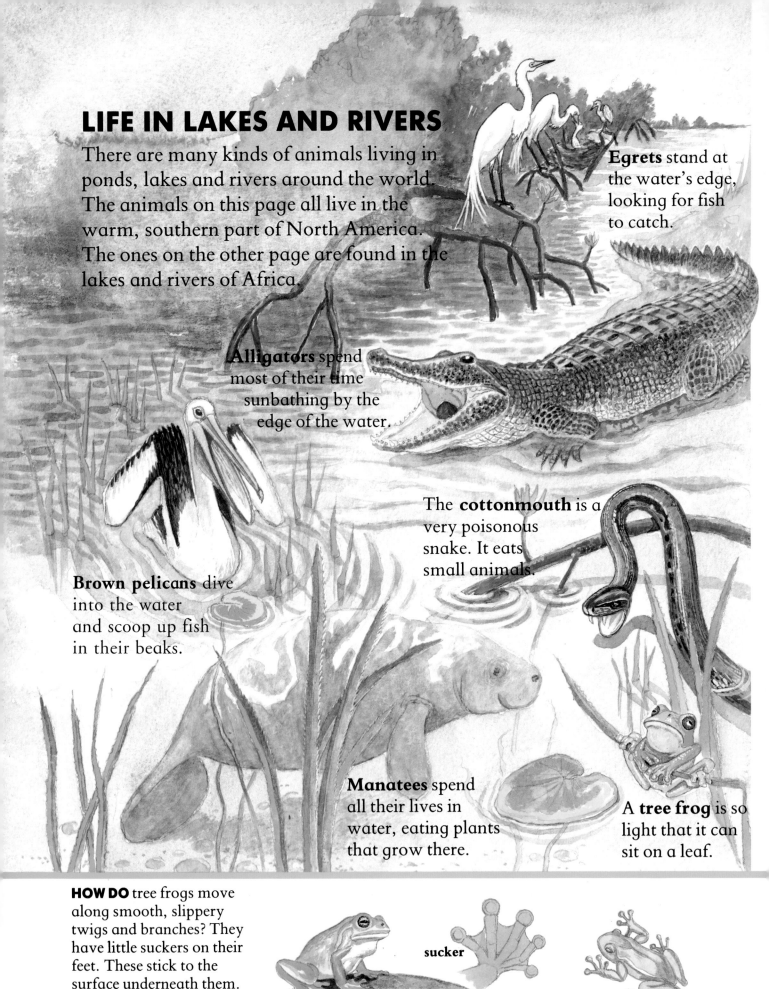

LIFE IN LAKES AND RIVERS

There are many kinds of animals living in ponds, lakes and rivers around the world. The animals on this page all live in the warm, southern part of North America. The ones on the other page are found in the lakes and rivers of Africa.

Egrets stand at the water's edge, looking for fish to catch.

Alligators spend most of their time sunbathing by the edge of the water.

The **cottonmouth** is a very poisonous snake. It eats small animals.

Brown pelicans dive into the water and scoop up fish in their beaks.

Manatees spend all their lives in water, eating plants that grow there.

A **tree frog** is so light that it can sit on a leaf.

HOW DO tree frogs move along smooth, slippery twigs and branches? They have little suckers on their feet. These stick to the surface underneath them.

sucker

Fish eagles are hunters. They eat mice and water birds as well as fish.

Crocodiles catch other animals when they come to the water to drink.

The **Goliath heron** lives by lakes, rivers, and the sea.

The **mouthbrooder** keeps its eggs and its young inside its mouth.

Jacanas are also called 'lily-trotters', because they can walk on water plants.

HOW DO crocodiles find their buried eggs? When the young are hatching, they cry. Their mother hears them and digs up the eggs so the young can get out. Then she carries them to the water, in her mouth.

ANIMALS OF AUSTRALIA

Many Australian plants and animals are different from those in other places. The trees are mostly a kind called eucalyptus. Many animals are marsupials. This means the mother has a pocket on her body, called a pouch. She carries her young in this.

Sugar gliders drink nectar from eucalyptus flowers. They glide from tree to tree.

Wombats stay in their burrows all day. They come out to graze at night.

Koalas eat only the leaves of eucalyptus. They hardly ever drink.

The **platypus** swims in rivers. It lays eggs in a burrow.

WHY DOES the male lyrebird dance? He shows off his tail and dances to warn other male lyrebirds to keep away. His tail feathers look like a musical instrument called a lyre.

These **kangaroos** are grass-eaters. They leap along on their back legs.

Dingos are wild dogs. They hunt rabbits and other animals.

Emus are very tall birds which cannot fly. Young emus are striped.

Mallee fowl keep their eggs warm by burying them in a pile of dead plants.

Dunnarts are also called 'marsupial mice'. They eat insects and other small creatures.

The **echidna** escapes from enemies by burying itself in the ground.

HOW DOES a tiny new-born kangaroo get into its mother's pouch? It climbs through its mother's fur to get there. It sucks milk and grows until it is big enough to leave.

37

MINIBEASTS

Many of the animals in the world are quite small ones, without backbones. They include insects, spiders, worms and other creatures that live in the soil. Some fly, and some creep along the ground. One name people sometimes give to all of these different animals is 'minibeasts'.

Mosquitoes bite people and other animals. They drink their blood.

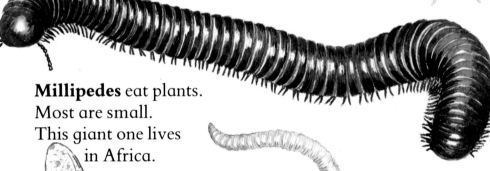

Centipedes have poisonous claws. They kill and eat other small animals.

Millipedes eat plants. Most are small. This giant one lives in Africa.

Earthworms eat dead plants. They drag these underground into their burrows.

Dragonflies lay their eggs in water. You can see dragonflies near streams.

Thousands of **ants** live together, looking after the queen ant and her eggs.

HOW DO butterflies grow?

They lay eggs on leaves. Caterpillars hatch.

They eat leaves and grow.

Each caterpillar becomes a chrysalis.

Inside this it becomes a butterfly.

It comes out.

It dries its wings and flies away.

The **garden spider** builds a web to trap insects.

Ladybirds are useful. They eat little insects called aphids, which damage plants.

The **garden snail** lives in cool, damp places. It eats plants.

Fireflies are beetles that glow in the dark. They live in hot countries.

Monarch butterflies live in North America. They fly south every autumn.

Bees make honey, to feed their young. People keep bees in hives.

HOW DOES a spider make a web?

It starts with one strand.

Then it makes more strands like the spokes of a wheel.

It weaves around the spokes.

39

AMAZING ANIMALS

This picture shows some unusual animals. Some are enormous. Others can run very fast, or travel long distances. Some have unusual ways of catching prey, or hiding from the enemies. Others just look rather strange or colourful.

There are many kinds of **birds of paradise**. The males have very beautiful feathers.

Komodo dragons are the biggest lizards of all. They can be three metres long.

Blue whales are the biggest animals that have ever lived. They can be 30 metres long.

Elephant seals are the biggest of all seals. They have trunks that look a bit like an elephant's.

Mudskippers are fish which crawl out of water on to tree roots.

HOW DO mudskippers stay out of the water? They take in air through their skins, but they cannot stay out of water for very long.

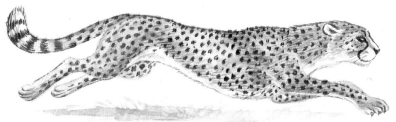

Cheetahs can run at more than 110 kilometres an hour.

The **skunk** drives enemies away by squirting them with horrible-smelling liquid.

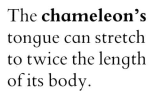

Bird-eating spiders are the biggest of all spiders – bigger than an adult person's hand.

Giant tortoises from the Galapagos Islands can be nearly a metre high.

The **chameleon's** tongue can stretch to twice the length of its body.

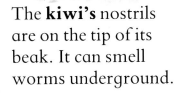

The **kiwi's** nostrils are on the tip of its beak. It can smell worms underground.

Geckos are little lizards. They can walk upside down on the ceiling.

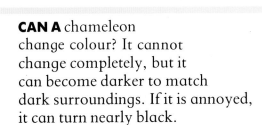

CAN A chameleon change colour? It cannot change completely, but it can become darker to match dark surroundings. If it is annoyed, it can turn nearly black.

41

ANIMALS IN DANGER

All over the world, there are animals in danger of dying out. People hunt and kill them, for meat or for fur. Sometimes people use the land where the animals live, and there is nowhere for the animals to go. Pollution is also very harmful to wildlife.

Ospreys eat fish. Pollution in the water harms the fish and the ospreys.

People have killed many **tigers** for their skins. Now they are rare.

Turtles lay their eggs on beaches. But people sometimes dig the eggs up.

Monk seals live in the Mediterranean sea. Pollution there harms the seals.

People cut down the forests where **orang utans** live.

HOW CAN animals be saved? Saiga antelopes on the grasslands of Asia were also hunted. When the hunting was stopped their numbers grew from a few hundred fifty years ago, to more than two million today.

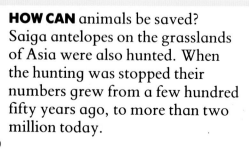

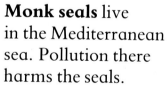

Giant otters live in Brazil. They are the rarest of all otters.

Gorillas live in African forests. Many are killed by hunters.

Kakapos are parrots from New Zealand. They cannot fly, so cats catch them.

Hunters have shot so many **Siberian white cranes** that there are very few left.

Pandas eat bamboo. In some places, this is dying, so the pandas have no food.

People kill **rhinoceroses** to get their horns. This is not allowed, but it still happens.

WHY DID the dodo die out? This large bird, from the island of Mauritius, could not fly. Sailors visiting the island killed so many dodos to eat that there were none left at all.

ANIMALS OF LONG AGO

The animals in this picture all lived on earth millions of years ago. They did not all live at the same time. Some of them are dinosaurs. The last of the dinosaurs died over 65 million years ago, but some had gone long before that.

This dinosaur belonged to a group called **hadrosaurs.** They had odd-shaped heads.

Tyrannosaurus was a hunter, which killed and ate other dinosaurs.

Ichthyosaurs were swimming reptiles. They had sharp teeth for catching fish.

Diatryma was a bird which did not fly. It was two metres tall.

Plesiosaurus was a reptile which swam in the sea and ate fish.

Iguanodon had front feet like hands and long back legs for running.

HOW LONG ago did these animals live?

Stegosaurus lived about 150 million years ago

Iguanodon lived about 120 million years ago

Ichthyosaurs lived about 200 million years ago

Triceratops' horns made it look fierce, but it ate only plants.

Brachiosaurus was one of the biggest animals that ever lived.

Hyracotherium was the first kind of horse. It was only about 30 centimetres tall.

Pterosaurs were flying reptiles. Some kinds were huge, and others were small.

Stegosaurus had spikes on its tail to protect it from meat-eating dinosaurs.

Dromiceiomimus had big eyes and a beak. It could run very fast.

Tyrannosaurus lived about 70 million years ago

Diatryma lived about 50 million years ago

People like us have been on the earth for about 100,000 years

45